Herding Goldfish: The Professional Content Marketing Writer in an Age of Digital Media and Short Attention Spans

By

Gene Knauer

1

Contents

Audience for this Book 6

1 - Introduction 7

    What is a Content Marketing Writer?...........................8

    Specializing 11

    Today's Attention Spans 12

    Content Marketing..13

2 - Positioning..15

    Positioning Statement 15

    Buyer Personas 18

    The Buyer's Journey...20

    The Elevator Pitch 21

3 - Types of Communications 24

    Blogs..25

    Collateral 29

    Email..30

    Sales Enablement Collateral 31

    Web Content...33

    Webinars..34

    White Papers...36

4 - Creative Techniques 39

    Establishing a Voice 40

    Rhythm and Tempo 45

    Clustering 46

    The Gestation Process of Ideas 49

    Authoring Templates 50

5 – Source Materials, Research, and Interviewing 54

    Source Materials 54

    Research 55

    Interviewing 57

6 - Writing Quality, Client Input, and Selling Your Services 61

    A Few Words on Style 62

    Content Optimization Software 63

    Client Input 65

    Dealing with Difficult Clients 66

    Measuring Your Effectiveness 67

    Marketing and Selling Your Services 68

Audience for this Book

Several audiences will find this book helpful. Anyone who is tasked with writing marketing communications for online, print, or broadcast media will find topics and guidance that could help them produce better work. Marketing communications professionals, product managers, and others who must write and produce sales and thought leadership content for products and services should find it useful, too. Students and those in transitional career stages who enjoy writing and are thinking about making a career of it will get an idea of what working as a content marketing writer might involve along with tips for working more efficiently, creatively, and successfully.

1 - Introduction

As long as we Homo sapiens communicate through the written word, writing as an occupation will employ millions of people around the world. Writing is essential for every type of marketing communication. Many people do it as a tangential job responsibility. For those who aspire to become content marketing writers, there's no one degree to obtain or clear career path to follow. The job requires writing skills, of course, and an understanding of the media, strategies, lifecycle, and techniques used for inbound and outbound marketing campaigns.

This book provides an overview of the what, how, and why of writing marketing communications. It includes marketing best practices written from the perspective of the content marketing writer; an overview of the kinds of communications you'll write; creative, research, and interviewing techniques; and advice on how to market your services—everything I could think of short of teaching you how to write. (There are a multitude of books and courses of study that do that extremely well.)

I got a university degree in journalism, became an advertising copywriter, wrote press releases and press kits for PR firms, and then the occasional freelance magazine article before I even knew that a career as a content marketing writer existed. I've been a content marketing writer ever since.

Over the years I've written thousands of communications and helped position dozens of companies. Often I get to see the impact and results of my efforts. When I began, I had no idea what a white paper was before I wrote one. A solution overview? Case study? Positioning statement? Elevator pitch? Data sheet? I had no idea what these things were either but have since learned how to master the art of writing them.

With the Web, new types of communications have gained prominence, like blogs and Web page content. This content is often consumed on mobile devices in our always-connected, multitasked, easily distracted lives. There is so much competing for our attention today that content that isn't short, punchy, and to-the-point risks being ignored. Of course editing out verbosity and crafting short sentences for maximum impacts have a long and distinguished history that predates the Web. The Ten Commandments, speeches by Winston Churchill and Abraham Lincoln, and most ad copy are excellent examples.

What is a Content Marketing Writer?

According to the American Marketing Association, marketing is "the activity, set of institutions, and processes for creating, communicating, delivering, and exchanging offerings that have value for customers, clients, partners, and society at large." Content marketing writers are responsible for the written communications used in marketing campaigns.

So basically, a content marketing writer helps sell things with words. These things can be products, services, concepts, political candidates, opinions, and on and on. At his or her best, the professional content marketing writer exercises:

- The skills of a journalist

- The facility to learn enough about a subject to write knowledgeably and with authority about it

- A creative yet precise writing style

- The patience and poise to work with difficult clients who are sometimes clueless about how to evaluate writing and work with a writer

Content marketing writers are sometimes referred to as copywriters, and these days "content writer" is the popular term. In the technology world, I've encountered many people who confuse the writing I do with technical writing. Technical writers create hardware and software documentation, online help, instructional manuals, and other sorts of technical documents—very different from what a content marketing writer is responsible for.

You don't get a byline for marketing writing. The rewards include the ability to work with words for a living, to get paid for it, and to take on diverse and interesting projects.

A 2015 survey by the employment search engine Web site Indeed.com found that the word "content marketing" in job postings has grown four-fold in recent years.

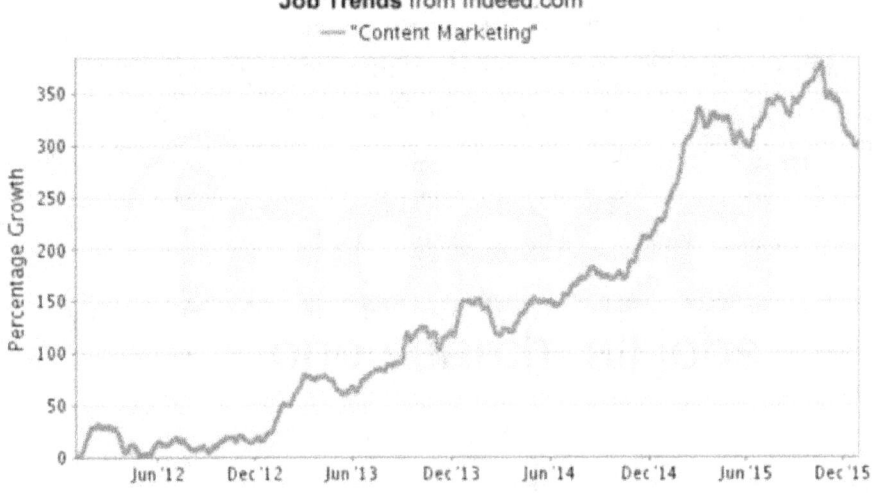

Job Trends from Indeed.com
—— "Content Marketing"

There were 136,500 marketing writing jobs in the United States in 2014. Two out of three content marketing writers were self-employed. The median pay was $58,850 a year or $28.30 per hour.[1] Based in the San Francisco Bay Area, my writer colleagues and I have earned quite a bit more than that annually.

The number of content marketing writers in the U.S. is probably much higher than the statistics above because, as previously mentioned, many people are responsible for writing marketing materials and their titles don't always include the word "writer". This goes for the rest of the world as well. A search of LinkedIn using "marketing" as the key word returned a total of over 10 million profiles globally for one researcher. So it's safe to assume that writing content marketing is a widespread activity.

Specializing

Many different industries use content marketing writers. You'll find people writing marketing communications content for healthcare, technology, science, finance, travel, education, and all sorts of professional services. Each industry has its own language, competitors, target customers, and market dynamics. Once you've gained a foothold with a client in one industry, you have an advantage over other writers who lack that industry experience. The more you do for that industry, the deeper your specialization grows. Often clients look for writers who understand and have experience working with their industry. So look to specialize in one or more area because it's an advantage you can exploit.

I'm a good example. I specialized in telecommunications. After working on advertising campaigns for retailers, a radio station,

---

[1] United States Department of Labor, Bureau of Labor Statistics, 2014.

hotels, condominium developments, packaged food companies, the SPCA, and miscellaneous others, I began getting writing work with technology companies. (Living in the San Francisco Bay Area — home to companies like Intel, Apple, Oracle, Facebook, Twitter, and a continual yearly crop of technology startups — this wasn't at all surprising.)

Among my earliest technology clients was Cisco Systems, the company whose founders developed the first commercial network router in a lab at Stanford University. I began by writing articles for their glossy company magazine. Then I was referred to one of the marketing departments and wrote a series of white papers on data center infrastructures for service providers. This was something I knew nothing about at the time. But by using my interviewing skills to question subject matter experts and product managers on each project, I began to understand enough conceptually to write about the products, technologies, competitors, and market. Cisco has since become the biggest networking company in the world. Those early products are shadows of what is available today as networks have morphed into the incredible backbone supporting nearly every facet of our lives.

I continue to write for Cisco and other technology companies. My nearly two decades of specialization has been invaluable. This expertise helps me to get new assignments and new clients, to conduct interviews with a base of historical and up-to-date knowledge, and to write with authority about a complex and dynamic industry.

Today's Attention Spans

Humans 8, goldfish 9—average attention span in seconds, that is.

In 2015, 2,000 people in Canada participated in a Microsoft study to measure attention spans. A similar study in 2000 found the average person typically focused on one thing for a maximum of 12 seconds. Fifteen years later, that number had declined to eight seconds, putting us below goldfish.

There are many theories for this increasing attention deficit. Foremost among them is that we have learned to multitask between the digital and real worlds. Millions of us each day routinely carry on a conversation while scanning our smartphone, eating, glancing at the TV, and preparing our dog's food all at the same time. (But even before all of the technology in our lives, any harried parent became adept at multitasking to handle cooking, shopping, cleaning, kids, work, spouse or significant other, and myriad other things.)

So content has to be written well and concisely or we move on. Make sure you have the right information. Write with a journalist's precision in the correct voice for the particular medium and audience. Add a dash of style. And don't be boring.

Content Marketing

Content marketing is a category of marketing you'll hear a lot about as a content marketing writer. It's often also referred to as "inbound marketing" which is a strategy for developing a relationship with prospects and customers through compelling communications that urge readers to respond through the Web. Marketers call content marketing a two-way relationship with customers because often the back-and-forth connection is ongoing. Inbound marketing is the Web-enabled response to the declining success of other types of marketing (such as direct mail, TV and radio ads, and cold calling) that has been labeled "outbound marketing".

For inbound content marketing campaigns, writers develop articles, blogs, white papers, how-to guides, social media posts, emails, seminars, and many other communications. Content is geared to the interests and needs of a company's prospects and customers. The words you write are the hook, line, and sinker to entice online eyeballs. In sales language, the goal of content marketing is to attract, convert, and close.

When you get an email offering a free e-book with new research on the benefits of breast feeding your baby from a company that sells disposal diapers, that's content marketing. To get the e-book you'll usually have to fill out a form with your contact information, which is then used for subsequent communications.

The strategy isn't new. Jell-O published and distributed a free cookbook in 1904 that promoted all sorts of recipes with Jell-O as a main ingredient. It was a huge success. More recently, Virgin Mobile created a social newsroom to promote apps, music, and other digital content to their wireless customers. The newsroom has become a source of revenue and a way to solidify Virgin's brand. The accounting and consulting firm Crowe Horwath focused a content marketing effort on financial institutions. It posted case studies, infographics, videos, and other communications with content of interest to these prospects. Almost 800 leads and several big new customers were the result.

Thousands of companies in diverse industries are creating content marketing campaigns for business-to-business and business-to-consumer products and services. Why is content marketing so popular these days? It's much less expensive than other forms of advertising and marketing. It can be targeted with great precision to the right audiences. And, if a company is providing compelling content, with flair, in the right channels, to the right people, content marketing can deliver impressive results.

2 - Positioning

The term "positioning" was coined in 1969[2] but people have been doing it for millennia. Vendors at open air village markets, traveling salesmen, corporate account managers, and online marketing executives all sell their company's wares successfully by having a keen sense of the need for what they're selling and pursuing a strategy for how best to sell it. As the famous business consultant and writer Peter Drucker wrote: "Every organization operates on a Theory of the Business…a set of assumptions as to what its business is, what its objectives are, how it defines results, who its customers are, what the customers value and pay for…"[3] This is positioning.

Positioning Statement

The ideas about the business contain the key data you need—the target audience, product or service name and features, market niche, unique benefits, and other information—to create a positioning statement. Positioning statements are often used in sales enablement materials to educate sales people on the what, how, and why of what's being sold. A well-written positioning statement

---

[2] "'Positioning' is a game people play in today's me-too market place," by Jack Trout, *Industrial Marketing Magazine*, June, 1969.

[3] "Management Challenges for the 21st Century," by Peter Drucker, Taylor & Francis Ltd., 1999.

should convey a distinctive identity that differentiates a product, service, institution, or even a person from everything else.

Sometimes the positioning statement is supplied to a content marketing writer for reference but I've been tasked with writing positioning statements from scratch as well. Here are the basic building blocks of a positioning statement.

ELEMENTS OF A POSITIONING STATEMENT

Audience	Defined at a higher level than an individual buyer persona (for example: institutional investors, regional governments, multi-national insurance companies, parents of autistic children).
Problem or Situation	This should clearly state the prospect's challenges, opportunities, or other situation that would lead to an interest in buying the product or service (for example: to be able to offer new services to customers, to counter competition, to reduce overhead, to increase the speed and quality of customer service, to decrease network downtime).
Product or Service Definition	A concise description of the product or service and its key features and benefits.
Value Proposition	Explains why this product or service is the very best choice among all options. Surprisingly, this very important element in positioning is often missing. The value proposition elegantly sums up the value that is being gained by the purchase.
Differentiation	What is truly unique about the product, service, company founders, company history, etc., that sets it apart from the

competition (for example: patents for a unique discovery, least expensive product, first on the market, fastest, best-selling, highest grossing, award-winning, only product with a particular features)?

The positioning statement is not usually used verbatim in marketing communications. Rather it is a collection of marketing intelligence to help write communications, qualify prospects, nurture customers throughout the buyer's journey, and continue the relationship after the sale.

Here is a sample positioning statement for a service. Remember that positioning statements do not usually result in elegant marketing writing because their role is to provide a briefing to sales and marketing staff with pertinent information in one paragraph.

SAMPLE POSITIONING STATEMENT FOR A SERVICE

Serious salt water aquarium owners care about the continued wellbeing of and significant investment in their fish and plants and understand that they are fragile and require continual expert care. The Aquarius Service provides a total setup and maintenance package. Our bi-weekly maintenance service includes the refill of automatic feeders, water changes, check of salinity levels, cleaning of all tank surfaces, and the assurance of the continued health and beautify of our customer's aquariums-—in homes, offices, and retail locations. Aquarius technicians can also help design aquariums and recommend custom or pre-built solutions, recommend compatible fish and plant combinations, and provide guidance on filtration, lighting, heating, food, and other products. Aquarius was voted top aquarium service vendor by the Pet Store Association of America for the past decade and has over 25,000 customers in North America.

Companies evolve and change and so do positioning statements. They should capture the up-to-date dynamics of the market, products, services, and competitors.

Buyer Personas

Know your customer. Know your audience. This is what the buyer persona is all about.

Think of the buyer persona as a character sketch, but instead of someone you'll write about in a story or a play, this is someone you'll write your content to appeal to. Today, marketing professionals have often already mapped out the persona or personas that characterize the buyers of their products and services before they'll hand you a writing assignment. You might be given a report containing a persona (or several personas) looking something like this:

James Kentfield, Furniture Operations Manager

Median Salary $108,000.
Average age: 48
Mostly male demographic

CATEGORY	DESCRIPTION	TAKEAWAYS
Who am I?	Responsible for all factory equipment (including process machinery and material handling equipment) in	A key decision-maker for robotics on the factory floor. The ultimate decision-maker, however, is the

		factory owner.
What issues keep me up at night?	The furniture business is struggling to stay afloat due to foreign competition. Greater efficiency to lower capital and operational costs must be achieved to gain decent margins and competitiveness. Knows that technology could help but he is nervous about replacing long-time employees and also is somewhat of a technophobe and Luddite.	Lead with the cost-efficiencies possible with our solutions. Give real return-on-investment examples. Talk about simplified processes. Be sensitive to the people issues factories are dealing with and their skepticism of technology, especially robotics.
Who do I buy from now?	There have been software companies in this market offering automation solutions but very little in the way of robotics.	Need to establish credibility in this market by appearing at industry gatherings, doing a proof-of-concept trial at a high-profile prospect.
Buying behavior	Prefers printed content and reports with detailed statistics on features, benefits, and cost savings.	Provide plenty of printed collateral and a customized assessment.

Who do I trust?	Colleagues, reports from the National Alliance of Furniture Crafters, and hands-on demonstrations.	Do an in-factory proof-of-concept demonstration. Speak at industry events. Sponsor a booth at industry tradeshows. Advertise in industry publications.

The persona has a title and sometimes even a name so you can better envision a real person. A background section describes what the person is responsible for and what buying authority he or she has. The demographics section can include an age range, gender, salary, education, values, and even what type of family the persona might have. The persona's goals and challenges are outlined. Possible objections to the marketing messages the company is promoting may also highlighted. And so on.

Sometimes buyer persona data can go on for more than one page. It may be based on focus groups conducted with the target audience. This data can include quotes from focus group participants, survey results, and even individual or group impressions of the product or service being marketed, a marketing message, or an elevator pitch.

Having data on target personas can be very valuable as you craft marketing communications. If you're selling graphic design software you're talking to one group of personas. If you're selling home remodeling services, laundry detergent, private jet rentals, enrollment in an anime conference, or network firewalls, you're addressing very different personas who will respond to different arguments delivered in different writing styles.

The Buyer's Journey

Package design, established brand identity, and signage help convince us to reach for a particular box of cereal or toothpaste when we're shopping at a supermarket. But with more complex products and services sold directly to consumers or between businesses, a more involved, multi-phase process of research and deliberation often precedes a purchase decision. This multi-phase process has been called the buyer's journey.

The basic phases of this decision-making journey include awareness, research, and the decision—otherwise referred to as attract, convert, and close. Specific marketing communications are developed for each stage.

MARKETING COMMUNICATIONS FOR PHASES OF THE BUYER'S JOURNEY

Phase 1. Awareness

Purpose: To gain awareness among prospects. Communications may link to a research or analyst report, registration for a seminar, or a free e-book. The goal is to get the prospect to pay attention, become intrigued, and to pursue their curiosity.

What you'll write: Email, blog, posts on social media, infographic, e-book.

Phase 2: Research

Purpose: To convince the customer that your product or service is what they're looking for. Communications should have a clear call to action for more information. A free Webinar, sales call, or in-person seminar event are other ways of educating prospects during this phase.

What you'll write: Web content with a lot of details, features, and benefits; white paper; podcast.

Phase 3: Decision

Purpose: To aid in the final decision. Product or service comparisons, customer experiences, and detailed collateral with features and benefits are useful during this phase.

What you'll write: Product comparison, benchmarking paper, case studies, trial download, and collateral.

The Elevator Pitch

For organized sales efforts, sales enablement materials such as sales playbooks, PowerPoint presentations, and competitive "battlecards" often contain an elevator pitch. This is nothing more than a sales pitch. The elevator ride is a metaphorical device for emphasizing that a sales pitch has to be short and to-the-point—it must be deliverable in the time it takes to ride with a prospect in an elevator.

Writing an elevator pitch is a great exercise in honing a sales message. It isn't meant to be recited verbatim but rather to give the sales person an idea of what elements a pitch for a particular product or service might include.

An elevator pitch will of course vary dramatically based on what is being sold, but here are the major elements.

Talk about the person's business, about the challenges they are likely confronting, to show that you understand what they're up against.

Let them know that a certain category of products or services exist to address these challenges.

Then mention the product or service that you're selling and why it is the best choice.

Suggest ways to further inform the prospect about the product or service, including literature, a demonstration, a seminar, a free evaluation or an analysis.

3 - Types of Communications

As a content marketing writer, you will be called on to write a variety of communications. Each is distinct, with different rules, structure, and intent. To be successful as a content marketing writer requires that you adapt your style to fit these different types of communications.

Blogs should have a fresh, conversational tone, almost as if you're listening to someone riff about a subject or an opinion. You can be funny, ironic, dramatic, or otherwise emotional in a blog. Web content and emails should be very to-the-point, with short sentences, bullets, and subheads helping to visually organize what you're trying to communicate for easier, faster reading. White papers are among the most formal of communications, organized to give an overview of what's being presented and then a logical flow to best communicate an involved subject. But that doesn't mean that they shouldn't be written with a fluid, compelling style to keep people reading.

All of these and other types of marketing communications must have a "call to action" or a way to respond for more information. This may include an email alias, a phone number, a form to fill out for a callback from a sales representative, a link to a product or collateral Web page, and so on. Sometimes the call to action is contained at the end of another piece of content (like a video or audio recording, infographic, or survey) that the first communication leads readers to. To make calls to action even more powerful, offers are associated with them (such as a special discount, free consultation, or free e-book).

Here are descriptions of some leading forms of marketing communications that you will be working on as a content marketing writer.

Blogs

The Weblog (now commonly known as a blog) is traditionally a short expository essay, often written in an informal, conversational style. Marketing blogs provide information, opinions, photos, videos, links to brand advertising, Web sites, and collateral. Most blogs allow the reader to leave comments, so the blog is a type of social networking. Microblogs are a shorter version of blogs, written for texting services such as Twitter.

I have ghost-written many blogs for executives in large corporations and small startup companies. These blogs were posted on company Web pages that featured blogs from folks throughout the company or on industry sites where blogs highlighted guest authors.

A great way to approach a blog assignment is to interview the person who has the information that the company wants to communicate, either in one or a series of blogs. The person to be interviewed is often not the same person whose name will be on the byline.

Ask enough questions to thoroughly understand what needs to be conveyed. Get any related materials needed to add details and to write with authority, such as research reports, statistics, press releases, and collateral. Then arrange your notes into a brief outline and send it to the client for approval. Once the outline is approved, the blog can be written with greater confidence.

Begin with a provocative, impactful headline because your first challenge is to entice people to read the blog. Then use multiple subheadings and visuals if any are available to divide short sections of text (perhaps two or three short paragraphs). Bullets and visuals are also very useful to help speed the reader along. Hyperlinks save you from having to explain certain terms or give the reader places to go for more information on complex concepts, people, associations, links to related blogs or a blog series, etc.

The informal nature of blogs makes them fun to write. They have always reminded me of a cross between copy for a radio or TV voiceover and a feature article. Writing a marketing blog is a great opportunity to show off your creativity.

Case Studies

Case studies are marketing collateral with perhaps the highest level of credibility because they tell real stories of how customers have benefited from products, services, partnerships, or whatever else your client is selling. The best case studies include clearly articulated quantitative and qualitative benefits and outcomes.

There are several types of case studies. External customer case studies require interviews with the internal sales team and whoever is representing the customer (which may include the person or persons who made the decision to buy the product or service, those who used it and noted its benefits firsthand, or an executive from the company as spokesperson). Since the customer is allowing their name to be used, they must sign off on the case study. Another variety of this customer case study does not name the customer but rather identifies the company generically (e.g., a leading, multinational financial services firm, a European pharmaceutical company, the leading North American paper recycler).

External customer case studies are usually displayed on the Web or printed and distributed in special mailings, at trade shows, and as part of presentations and proposals. You'll write them based on this basic outline:

- A headline that captures the highlights of the story much like a newspaper article or press release

- Overview of the customer's business and market

- Challenge or need that prompted the customer to look for the product or service

- How the customer became aware of the product or service and learned how it addresses their needs better than anything else available

- Benefits derived by the customer, either quantitative (such as lower total cost of ownership, higher return on investment, lower operational or capital expenditures, higher revenue generated, or lower customer churn) or qualitative (such as more positive customer perceptions of a brand, a more user-friendly interface, or observations that the customer has gained greater efficiencies)

Internal-only case studies for sales, sometimes called win stories, are written from the perspective of the successful account manager, account team, or other salesperson. These case studies capture the tactics and historical record that led up to a sale and are meant to help other sales people replicate the successful strategy.

You'll be writing sales-oriented case studies using this basic outline:

- A headline that captures the highlights of the story much like a newspaper article or press release

- Overview of the customer's business and market

- How the opportunity was uncovered by the salesperson or sales team

- What the customer was grappling with that made it a good prospect for the product or service

- How the sales team educated the customer, competed with rivals, priced the offering, or used other creative tactics to win the sale

- When the sale occurred and how much revenue was generated

- How the customer has benefitted from the product or service

These sales-focused case studies are available on internal company intranets alongside sales enablement collateral. Sometimes the contact information of the account manager or others on the sales team is made available so other salespeople can contact them for more information.

Collateral

Brochures, data sheets, solution briefs, presentations, white papers—these and other types of written media fall under the category of collateral. They are made available to read or view on the Web, as a download, or as printed pieces. Sophisticated, well-written collateral isn't a replacement for salesmanship but collateral is used in every marketing campaign to amplify the sales message.

Writing collateral requires the same basic information as other marketing writing projects. Information on the product or service to be sold and the personas of target customers is necessary. An understanding of how the collateral will be used is also important because different calls to action may be required. For example, a presentation that is part of a content marketing campaign might end with an email address or phone number for more information while the same presentation on a Web page might instead lead to a survey or an immediate callback button.

Finally, an understanding of the format for each type of collateral is important so you know, for example, the maximum word count per section, where to use subheads, whether you can incorporate visuals, and whether scripting for a presentation is required.

Email

Most of us complain about getting too much email full of unsolicited spam and irrelevant information and offers, right? Perhaps. But according to a 2015 survey by MarketingSherpa, 72% of consumers consider email their favored media for receiving information from companies they do business with. Of these consumers, 61% said they like to receive weekly promotional emails.

The Direct Marketing Association claimed in 2013 that 66% of consumers make purchases online as a direct result of seeing an email marketing message. For business-to-business marketing, email is perhaps the single most popular marketing communications tool, with 80% of marketing departments using it, according to a 2014 research study by the Content Marketing Institute.

So email isn't going away anytime soon—despite efforts by productivity software vendors like Slack and Dropbox to replace it with collaborative portals. Plan on mastering email communications as a content marketing writer. It's a highly competitive medium and you're going to have to know what you're doing to be successful.

Email is highly personal; it's like leaving a voicemail message for an individual. With an understanding of the target market and possible buyer personas, marketing emails should be welcoming, clearly address the needs of the recipient, and motivate an action. There are many aspects to successful email marketing, from the list to the design, but I'm just focusing here on what the writer is responsible for.

The email subject line is the grabber, the words that the recipient will see to make the decision to delete or open your email. To get people to do the latter, the subject line should be clever, enticing, and attention-getting. Here are some examples of subject lines that might induce someone to open an email, depending upon the audience:

Kiss your blow dryer goodbye

When is Father's Day again?

You wore that to work?

FREE study on interval training for upper body strength

Your subscription is expiring

2-DAY SALE - 80% off all Nike running shoes

Recommended just for you

Be welcoming and respectful in your email body copy. Get to the point quickly. The clock is ticking and you could lose the reader at any point. Add relevant content to your sales message (such as a photo, video, link to a Web page or to social media). Create excitement. A sense of urgency can be conveyed if an offer is ending soon or available for a limited time. And include a clear call-to-action in the email (for example, click on a link to find out more, shop, sign up, compare, register, download, or otherwise respond). Some marketers also make a point of encouraging customer feedback to emails and other communications. This forges a dialogue with customers and gives marketers data used to fine-tune elements of marketing campaigns and even products and services.

Sales Enablement Collateral

A subset within the collateral category is known as sales enablement collateral. It is specifically focused on arming sales people with the marketing media they need to effectively win business at each phase of the buyer's journey. For an insurance agent, this might include brochures, a printed folder to hold proposals, and a PowerPoint presentation that can be delivered onsite to a customer or prospect. For account managers selling technology products to corporate IT departments, sales enablement collateral might include data sheets, feature comparison papers contrasting their product with those of competitors, and case studies.

In addition, training content may be included among sales enablement collateral deliverables. There are also battlecards, which are one-page cheat sheets containing product positioning messaging, the value proposition, competitive comparisons, target personas, and other details that sales should keep top-of-mind when approaching or presenting to prospects.

Sales playbooks are more detailed, strategic collections of information for a sales campaign. They often include market research, details about the sales opportunity, customer personas, customer challenges, competitor positioning, selling strategies, details on working with partners to close the deal, cross-sell and up-sell opportunities, product and services information, prospecting questions, prospect objections that might be raised and how to counter them, and resource contacts to help with financing, support, shipping, manufacturing, demonstrations, and so on.

Content marketing writers are sometimes asked to create these communications. Such projects require the writer to collect a lot of information often from different people in different departments within a company. Getting input and feedback from sales people is also vital as they are the ones approaching and presenting to customers regularly and know what materials and strategies work best.

Web Content

Writing for the Web requires a staccato tempo. You're competing against short attention spans and the urge to point-and-click away. Say it quickly. Clearly. Use headlines and bullets to break up blocks of text.

Many Web sites today have been designed to cater to mobile users. There are single pages that you can scroll down to see, one at a time, or Pinterest-style card or grid-based layouts like Google+

with different widgets in separate boxes. Writing for mobile-oriented Web sites requires even shorter bits of content. A good way to think of each page is like a separate ad, with a headline, visual, and some body copy. Many of the new mobile Web sites strive to be very interactive, so you're continually prompted to click a button that takes you to another Web page for more information, to watch a video, to download collateral, to shop, or to request a contact from a company representative.

When you're writing content for more traditionally designed Web sites, word counts are higher but the need to be short and to-the-point remains. Web sites are a highly visual marketing medium so try to let visuals communicate instead of words wherever possible.

Search engine optimization (SEO) is something you'll encounter when writing for the Web. Consumers researching products and services online do so by typing key words into search engines, so marketers want their Web sites to appear near the top of these search results. To do so, they strive to understand what these key words are and to and use them in Web content to help "optimize" that content for search engines.

Often clients will give you a list of key words to include. You might also hear the term "long tail keywords" and this refers to a three-word or longer key word phrase used repeatedly for particular searches.

Webinars

A marketing webinar is a presentation, seminar, or class held on the Web using a conferencing application such as Join.me, GoToMeeting, or WebEx. Webinars have become popular marketing tools to inform customers, partners, and prospects about a company's products, services, news, changes in partner programs, and other miscellaneous topics.

For the content marketing writer, working on a webinar usually includes either creating a presentation (often using Microsoft PowerPoint or something equivalent) from scratch, slide by slide, or scripting a presentation already created. Creating a webinar presentation from the beginning requires the involvement of a subject matter expert (from whom you'll get the content) and a graphic designer or presentation specialist (who will create the visuals in the slides).

A great way to draft the initial content and story flow for a webinar presentation is to use the same sort of template used to write a video script. There are two columns: the left column contains the script to be delivered by the presenter, the right column contains the visuals and titles, bullets, and other text to be contained in the corresponding slide. At the initial stage, you might include a description of the visual as a direction to the artist.

You'll work with the subject matter expert on the story flow. I've found that one of the most effective ways to organize a webinar presentation that features a product or a service is to use the elements of an elevator pitch as a guide. After the presenter's introduction that includes his or her name, the topic of the webinar, and the agenda, consider following this format:

- Overview of industry, market, situation, or opportunity that is leading to the need for a particular product or service (statistics from third party sources are highly credible and good to include)

- Features that are needed in a product or service to meet the challenge or respond to the opportunity (present these generically before introducing the company's product or service)

- A description of the product or service that provides the solution (a product or service overview with features and benefits)

- Factors that make this the very best choice for customers (such as industry awards, patents, leader in a market category, sales volume, major customers, benchmark results)

- What additional information is available about the product or service (call-to-action may include scheduling an appointment with a sales rep, arranging for a demo or product trial, getting more detailed information in collateral, or how to purchase the product or service)

Marketing webinars can be about a variety of things other than direct selling, from company news to market briefings, changes to partnership programs, product roadmaps, product end-of-life announcements, etcetera. So content and topic organization will therefore vary.

If you are simply tasked with writing a script for a presentation that has already been created (the script is usually placed in the notes pages of a PowerPoint presentation so that anyone can deliver the presentation with the approved content), set up a time to interview the person who is responsible for creating and presenting the webinar. Have them deliver the presentation to you and record it or take notes to capture the delivery. Ask questions when something isn't clear or doesn't make sense.

Some people are very good at speaking extemporaneously while others tend to go off on tangents or are too verbose. The content marketing writer can add great value to script writing, trimming content to get right to the point, with a bit of flair but moving the presentation along briskly to maintain the audience's attention and interest. The marketing guru and author Guy Kawasaki, former chief evangelist of Apple, believes in the 10-20-30 Rule as optimal for presentations: 10 slides, 20 minutes maximum, 30 point font is the smallest font to use. This is of course only a recommendation. The point is to keep it as short as possible and to-the-point.

White Papers

The white paper is used in marketing to present complex value propositions, usually in 10 to 20 pages—sometimes more, sometimes less. White papers written to establish "thought leadership" might not actually sell anything but rather present advice about a topic or trend to establish credibility for the sponsoring organization. This marketing communication is a particularly excellent choice for promoting things like technology, scientific products, government policy, and services.

The well-written white paper presents the business case and market for a product, service, policy, strategy, or other topic. The paper then describes the key concept clearly and concisely, with illustrative visuals and a minimum of marketing hype. Write white papers with an authoritative journal article in mind. That doesn't mean the style should be formal and fussy but that topics should be fully and clearly explained; any statistics or forecasts cited should have source attribution; and explaining something complex to your readership comes across as the main thrust of the paper.

The structure of the marketing white paper includes:

- A title, no byline

- A one or two-paragraph abstract or executive overview section that gives the reader a quick snapshot of what the paper will cover

- An introductory or overview section that provides some context (e.g., an industry situation, a public health predicament) and the paper's thesis (e.g., "...your data center needs Flash-based storage media to protect your critical data assets and better serve your dynamic IT environment" or "...national service should be a mandated two-year requirement for every 19-year-old because our country will gain a needed workforce to handle overdue public-sector infrastructure projects and service will be a valuable lesson in the duty and privilege of citizenship for young people").

- A middle section (varying tremendously based on subject matter) that contains details on the topic and research data, visuals, tables, case studies, use cases, etcetera

- A closing section that summarizes the key points presented in the white paper, including a soft-sell marketing message from the company, and a call-to-action for more information

Writing an outline for a white paper is a very prudent idea. I've worked on projects where the outline served as a way for clients to figure out what they wanted me to present. These meetings turned into brainstorming sessions. The subsequent outline drafts helped clients think through their marketing messages. By the time they signed off on the outline—sometimes after eight or more versions—they were much clearer about what they wanted. And when I delivered the first drafts, they knew what to expect so revisions were relatively minor.

There are many other types of marketing communications you may be asked to write. Podcasts, videos, e-books, newsletters, and infographics are some examples. In each case, study existing content to get a sense of the format and style required. Then use the same prism to understand who you're selling to, what you're selling, and how to sell it that you use for all marketing writing projects.

4 - Creative Techniques

The experience of reading through content marketing on the Web can sometimes feel like watching a spaghetti western because you're confronted with the good, the bad, and the ugly. There is great content out there. But all too often you'll encounter wildly varying levels of marketing writing proficiency—even within the same company's content—and a lot of repetition and sameness.

A lot of product collateral starts with a laundry list of a features and benefits instead of first addressing the customer's needs and the product's value proposition. Overly complex descriptions confuse instead of clarify. Long sentences in dense paragraphs test a reader's patience and perseverance. Poorly written content marketing lacking originality, creativity, organization, and precision isn't just an editorial headache. It can degrade a brand's credibility. Worse, it can stop the buyer's journey cold, reducing response rates and bottom line revenue.

Here are some stylistic elements that contribute to great content marketing. Also included in this chapter are techniques to jumpstart brainstorming and the creative process. Finally, the use of authoring templates, which can be extremely useful, is discussed.

Establishing a Voice

We pay attention to actors in movies, characters in books, and public figures with distinctive personalities, interesting things to say, and intriguing ways of saying them. They stand out from the nameless, bland crowd. Well-written content marketing with a distinctive voice can do the same thing. Aside from all of the visual tools that marketing communications has to draw on, voice in writing is a powerful element you can use to help more impactful writing and a stronger brand identity.

Too few companies use a distinctive voice to their advantage and many don't understand how best to use one consistently in their communications. If you start with a persona to focus on, it's easier to remember that with every communication you're having a conversation with another person. Your writing voice should convey a general impression of friendliness, intelligence, and confidence. That doesn't mean you can't have a little fun as well.

Here are some examples of the use of a voice in marketing writing. Consumer product communications are full of great examples of distinctive voices. Below is copy for the J. Peterman Company catalogue. The voice is high-brow, tongue-in-cheek pretentious, recalling an entry in a woman's diary.

Creating Interest.

She's flown in a hot air balloon over the Grand Canyon.

Led a search for Bigfoot.

Camped out in the mountains of El Salvador.

A party isn't a party unless she's on the list.

Told Oprah, not this month.

She's...

Well, the truth is, I spotted this unusually interesting jacket on a woman walking through the lobby of "the" hotel in New York City.

And just imagined the rest.

(It was that interesting.)

Built in cache.

A good thing to have going for you. Curved Placket Jacket (No. 2658). After much searching I tracked it down in Paris, at one of those exclusive shops that Homeland Security is studying as a model. Creatively cut jacket is a bit shorter. Ottoman weave cotton for texture. Curved full-button placket accentuates the positive. Flattering princess seams. Fully lined. Unusual center back pleat to make you look as interesting going as coming. Imported.

I'm sure you can pick up hang gliding in no time.

From the J. Peterman Company Owner's Manual No. 137

And here is a portion of a JetBlue infographic with a distinctive, friendly, voice, even though the email is bugging people about not responding to previous promotional emails.

From JetBlue

Distinctive voices in business-to-business (B2B) marketing can also be very effective. This Web content for Ericsson is addressing corporate chief information officers, chief technology officers, and other executives responsible for building and maintaining data center infrastructure in large organizations. These buyers respond to authoritative vendors that understand the issues they're grappling with, who don't mince words and get to the point. Note that the majority of the content focuses on customer challenges and what is needed to meet those challenges. Only the last line mentions what is being sold.

INDUSTRIALIZE AND ACCELERATE

Today's datacenters are inflexible and inefficient. Way overprovisioned. Burdened with rigid products, technologies, and architectures.

The problem: the infrastructure is dictating the business, instead of the other way around.

It's time to say goodbye to traditional IT infrastructure.

Say hello to the new era of digital industrialization. To a datacenter designed as a digital factory: hyperscalable, software-defined, automated, and accessible in a way that you've never seen before.

This revolution requires us to look through a different lens and imagine what is possible. The time is now: either you change the game or the game changes you! This is the Networked Society, and it is bringing major opportunities, together with daunting challenges: the explosion of data, advanced analytics, new digital technologies, the Internet of Things, 5G, mobile networks.

With Ericsson Cloud, we are laying the foundations required for digital industrialization:

From the Ericsson Cloud Web site

And below is the About Us (in this case just 'us') Web page for UK-based juice manufacturer Innocent. Even the way the pages are listed and the lack of capitalization contribute to a friendly, honest tone of voice.

hello, we're innocent

...and we're here to make it easy for people to do themselves some good (whilst making it taste nice too).

We started innocent in 1999 after selling our smoothies at a music festival. We put up a big sign asking people if they thought we should give up our jobs to make smoothies, and put a bin saying 'Yes' and a bin saying 'No" in front of the stall. Then we got people to vote with their empties. At the end of the weekend, the 'Yes' bin was full, so we resigned from our jobs the next day and got cracking.

Since then we've started making coconut water, juice and kids' stuff, in our quest to make natural, delicious, healthy drinks that help people live well and die old.

Innocent Drinks Web site

Voice can even be used in legalese. Apple is famous for its distinctive advertising voice and design. That "Think Different" brand voice is evident even in the wording of its sales and refund policy.

U.S. Sales and Refund Policy

Thanks for shopping at Apple. We appreciate the fact that you like to buy the cool stuff we build. We also want to make sure you have a rewarding experience while you're exploring, evaluating, and purchasing our products, whether you're at the Apple Online Store, in an Apple Retail Store, or on the phone with the Apple Contact Center (To make it visually easier on both of us, we'll refer to these entities as the 'Apple Store' in this policy.)

As with any shopping experience, there are terms and conditions that apply to transactions at an Apple Store. We'll be as brief as our attorneys will allow. The main thing to remember is that by placing an order or making a purchase at an Apple Store, you agree to the terms set forth below along with Apple's Privacy Policy and Terms of Use.

Apple Web site

Rhythm and Tempo

The actor Christopher Walken is known for the odd way he delivers his lines. The tempo is unique. He speeds up, pauses, and accents words in unexpected syllables. Contrast that with the smooth delivery of a narrator in a training video.

We all have very sophisticated ears when it comes to the rhythm and tempo of written, sung, and spoken language. According to the Merriam-Webster Dictionary, *rhythm* is "an ordered recurrent alternation of strong and weak elements in the flow of sound and silence in speech." And *tempo* is "the rate of speed of a musical piece or passage."

Here is a superb and powerful example of the use of rhythm and tempo in writing. It's an excerpt from a famous speech given by Winston Churchill to the British people during the London Blitz bombings of World War II. There is a repetitive pace like a drumbeat, building until the last long sentence.

We shall not flag nor fail. We shall go on to the end. We shall fight in France. We shall fight on the seas and the oceans. We shall fight with growing confidence and growing strength in the war. We shall defend our own island whatever the cost may be.

We shall fight on the beaches. We shall fight on the landing grounds. We shall fight in the fields and in the streets. We shall fight on the hills. We shall never surrender; and even if, which I do not for a moment believe, this island or a large part of it were subjugated and starving, then our empire beyond the seas, armed and guarded by the British fleet, would carry on the struggle, until, in God's good time, the New World, with all its power and might, steps forth to the rescue and liberation of the old.

Consider using rhythm and tempo in writing marketing communications. It will set the material apart artfully and elevate you as an artist to the client.

Clustering

Natalie Goldberg, the author of the book *Writing Down the Bones: Freeing the Writer Within*, believes that talent is "like a water table under the earth—you tap it with your effort and it comes through you." She distinguishes between people in "monkey mind" (where we get overwhelmed by all of the noise and stimuli around us, which can block the ability to think freely and creatively) and "wild mind" (a vast, rich resource that you could think of as the way the unconscious is described in western psychology). Tapping into your wild mind isn't just useful for artists, musicians, poets and novelists. It's creative catnip for the content marketing writer too.

Clustering is a fun, creative, and effective technique to help engage your wild, creative mind. Here's how it works. Beginning with a central word or phrase related to what you're working on, write it in the center of a page and surround it with a bubble.

homelessness

Then add words or phrases that come to mind related to the central word. Group related words or phrases together. These form a branching structure that produces clusters of sub-categories.

Clustering allows you to think in words, to explore related and tangential words, phrases, and ideas freely. It's great for thinking of product names, headlines, ideas, titles, and virtually any concept.

The cluster above was done as part of brainstorming for an actual project, an ad that I worked on *pro bono* for a nonprofit organization that provides services to the homeless in Berkeley,

California. I used clustering to come up with headline. Here was the result.

Invisible Man

Every night in Berkeley, an average of 1100 men, women and children are homeless on our streets and need help. These men are our face of homelessness. The homeless are teenage runaways and battered women. They are the mentally ill and emotionally impaired. And they are the working poor who can't afford housing.

Since 1972, the Berkeley Emergency Food and Housing project (BEFHP) has been working to make sure the homeless are not invisible. BEFHP's mission is to not only ease the crisis of homelessness, but to end it. We are part of a national coalition to end homelessness in 10 years by moving people into transitions, jobs and housing.

Don't pretend they're invisible. Become a supporter of BEFHP today.

BERKELEY EMERGENCY FOOD AND HOUSING PROJECT
(510) 649-4965 EXT. 314

Now try it yourself. Let's say you're searching for a provocative headline for a white paper or a subject line for an email company. Pick a word at random (for example your name, your pet's name, the town where you live) and write it down. Then start adding words as they come to mind. If there is a word related to another word, connect the two together. See how many words or phrases you can come up with in five minutes. Turn off your inner editor and let the words flow in a stream-of-consciousness.

When you're finished with all of the words arrayed in front of you, see if you can come up with that headline or subject line.

The Gestation Process of Ideas

Marketing writing requires information, writing skills, and creative ideas. Sometimes those ideas flow freely while you're typing away. At other times, the way to begin a document, organize information, describe a complex product feature, or capture a value proposition is more elusive. It's important to remember that ideas often come to us in disjointed bits and pieces instead of the linear order that a document requires.

So get used to collecting the pieces of ideas.

Along with the piecemeal way that we get ideas, thinking and writing well involve a gestation process that includes the interplay between thinking, writing, and crafting. The average person has about 70,000 thoughts a day or 48.6 thoughts per minute, according to research by the Laboratory of Neuro Imaging at the University of Southern California. Beyond thinking with clarity, writing well is the process of making choices about what is preferable among options of how best to present information. The gestation process gives your conscious and unconscious time to come up with the right answers. Get used to listening for these thoughts as they come and capturing them.

One idea might be a way of describing something in a white paper. Another might be positioning for a company slogan, headline, or an idea for an article. In between you might think of the perfect gift for your spouse's birthday, an item you forgot to include on a shopping list, or about a great book topic. I tend to whip out my smartphone when inspiration strikes and dictate the ideas immediately.

Authoring Templates

One way to begin instituting company-wide is to through the use of authoring templates. These are Word templates that clearly define the elements required for each section of different types of communications, whether a Web page, brochure, data sheet, white paper, or other marketing assets.

Authoring Template: Brochure

Purpose: Brochures should provide customers with a detailed overview of our products or services.

Length and style: Try to keep to a maximum of four pages and 3000 words. Less is better. Be sure to address the customer directly as "you" and keep clichés and complex words out of your copy. See the corporate style guide if you have any questions.

See Donaldson CorpJet samples here.

Project Information:

Product Manager:

Writer:

Project Coordinator:

Production Manager:

Vendor (if relevant):

Due date:

Headline

Instructions: Name of product/solution/service + benefit

Word count: 10 words max (100 characters)

Example: Donaldson CorpJet is the Ultimate Executive Perk

Cover Visual

Instructions: Include in top half of first page. Should always show a customer enjoying the service.

Introduction

Instructions: Lead with customer challenges that would be addressed with CorpJet service. Try to grab the reader by letting them know that we understand their business issues related to business travel. Cite statistics where possible to enhance credibility. (Maximum 200 word count for this section.)

Benefits Sidebar

Instructions: Include Donaldson CorpJet service benefits. May vary based on the different vertical markets we serve. Maximum of five bullets.

Example: Time-to-cost ratio savings of 65%

Body

Instructions: Describe the Donaldson CorpJet service in detail. (Maximum 1500 word count for this section.)

CorpJet Mission Statement

Instructions: Include our latest mission statement, which differentiates our service from competitors. (Maximum 1500 word count for this section.)

Contacts

Instructions: Include corporate sales phone number. Leave blank box for individual sales person to write in personal contact info.

5 – Source Materials, Research, and Interviewing

Content marketing writers come to the profession from many backgrounds. Journalists are trained to do research and conduct interviews but those skills may be new to others tasked with writing marketing communications. This chapter provides a brief overview of how to review source materials to make sure you have what you need to tackle an assignment, evaluate research you're given and supplement it with research you do on your own to strengthen your writing, and interview people most effectively.

Source Materials

Sometimes you're given everything you need to begin work on a marketing communications assignment. More often, however, the information required to write a complete, compelling argument for why someone should purchase something is incomplete. So step one at the beginning of an assignment is to do an information triage. With a critical journalist's eye, review the materials you've been given to determine what is useful, what is superfluous, and what information is missing.

I've been given many assignments by people who assured me that everything I needed was included in what they sent. Early on, I was reluctant to question that. I didn't want to appear inexperienced or confused. Not surprisingly, the drafts I submitted on those assignments were incomplete.

It is incumbent on the writer to press the client for correct, complete information. Be clear about what gaps you think exist. Without a clear value proposition, positioning, features and benefits, target audience, data to back up claims, and information about a product or service, your work will be flawed. If you don't speak up early on, you will be held accountable for a deficient draft and suffer the consequences.

In the review of raw content at the beginning of an assignment is where you can add real value as a writer. Many, if not most, people I work with need help not only in writing marketing materials but in knowing what information to gather and how to organize it. Beyond the actual writing work, this is another facet of your role as a content marketing writer where you can really make your mark.

Research

In journalism, research data commands far more credibility than claims and superlatives. So it is with marketing communications. Often companies sponsor research with a third-party research organization on topics related to their products or services. In-house research is also conducted. This may include focus groups or online surveys with customers, partners, and sales representatives.

Research companies that specialize in particular sectors—such as technology, energy, healthcare, insurance, and financial services—provide reports on a subscription basis. And then there is a lot of research in the public domain.

Ideally, market research should be gathered long before a marketing communications project is conceived and launched. It should provide insight or validation to:

- Bolster a company's assumptions about who their target customers are

- Uncover the key personas to focus on

- Understand the nature of customer challenges

- Scope out the marketplace for the company's products or services

- Compile a list of competitors, their offerings, and their strengths and weaknesses

- Propose ways to position the company to sell more successfully

- Foresee coming trends that the company can exploit

It is your job to determine whether individual data points are relevant to each writing assignment. If the data doesn't strengthen your selling argument, search for data that does. Marketing departments often receive a lot of research that may be useful to inform strategic decisions and tactics but may be less useful as quotable content in marketing materials. It's sometimes left up to you to make this determination and to explain why.

Additionally, you can do your own research in the public domain to bolster specific claims or comparisons. Be prepared to do a lot of sifting through Web and other content in reports and articles with a critical eye. Consider how credible each source is and make sure to attach attribution—the source—to every data point you include in your writing. Aside from citing numbers, look for qualitative data such as statements from experts on trends, markets, observations, anecdotes, and other things.

As mentioned, companies often use focus groups and surveys to better understand the needs and attitudes of customers, partners, and even employees such as sales representatives. This information can be incredibly valuable. The success of sales enablement collateral meant to be used by salespeople, for example, should be judged not only by how well it informs the end customer but by how useful sales personnel determine it is. Focus groups and surveys help marketing departments understand what collateral salespeople prefer, what content is most useful, and how best to make the collateral available to attract and inform established customers and prospects during each phase of the buyer's journey.

Interviewing

Whether you're interviewing a movie star about a role, a politician about a policy decision, a customer about their experience with a product, or a subject matter expert about a new technology, the basics of interviewing remain the same. A great article in the Columbia Journalism Review[4] captured these best practices nicely. Here are the main points, with comments based on my experiences as an interviewer added:

- **Know your subject**—or at least review all of the materials you've been given prior to the interview to

---

[4] "The Art of the Interview: Asking the Hard Questions about Asking the Hard Questions," by Ann Friedman, *The Columbia Journalism Review*, May 30, 2013.

determine what you know and what you don't know and need to come away from the interview understanding.

- **Write questions**—but as the interview progresses, allow yourself to be flexible enough to change the order of your questions, add new ones, and throw out others.

- **Embrace pauses in the conversation**—because I've found that by giving the person being interviewed time to collect his or her thoughts at intervals, they can sometimes dig deep and come out with articulate answers and interesting insights that would have been missing if I moved too swiftly to the next question.

- **Sometimes it's very effective to play dumb**—so if you have a little knowledge about something, don't rely on it but instead encourage the person you're interviewing to explain it to you as if you know next to nothing so you can get a complete overview rather than bits of the answer.

Take charge of the interview from the beginning. If the person you're interviewing is overly verbose or goes off on tangents that won't be useful to you, politely interrupt and get the conversation back on track. This is totally appropriate because this is your interview. The clock is ticking. Once your time is up, if the interview is incomplete, you're out of luck—unless you can schedule another interview.

Interviewing multiple people at once can be problematic. One way to handle this is to understand from the beginning each person's role and what information they are adept at talking about. If you're writing a customer case study about a software product, for example, perhaps one person is the executive decision maker and another is the technical lead who installed the product and a third person is an end user. Divide your interview into thirds and ask each person questions related to their different role and experience with the product.

When you're interviewing, ask as many questions as you deem necessary until you thoroughly understand what you're writing about. Don't be shy! A lack of understanding will come through in your writing like an unsightly stain. If the person you're interviewing does a poor job of explaining something, tell them that you still don't get it and don't let up until you do. Ask for examples to illustrate complex topics or concepts. If they throw out buzzwords that are unintelligible, let them know that it's Greek to you and insist that they translate. If their heavy accent makes it hard to decipher certain words, stop them and make sure that they enunciate clearly until you do understand.

Whenever possible, record the interview. Even if you type or scribble very fast, having to do so takes part of your concentration away from asking questions and listening to the answers intently.

At the end of the interview, always ask if you've covered everything. Surprisingly, I've found that when I ask this question people I'm interviewing often have a lot more to add, bringing up things I didn't think of or know to ask that have proven to be valuable fodder for my writing.

6 - Writing Quality, Client Input, and Selling Your Services

Once when I was a junior copywriter working at an advertising agency, to my everlasting shame I misspelled *hors d'oeuvres* in a brochure for a restaurant located in a client hotel. I can still picture the account manager's expression when he confronted me with the error after the expensive brochures had been printed. It wasn't pretty.

So always spell check every draft you submit for review. As client edits accumulate and you generate multiple drafts, spell check and review multiple times.

Read your final document start to finish in its last draft form. Especially when many people provide input, you may find that certain sections or words may sound a bit disjointed or like different, discordant voices. Additional last-minute tweaks are then necessary.

Always format your document properly, following the document styles for whatever you're producing. Using an authoring template that provides precise directions is a welcome guide for the writer.

A Few Words on Style

Writing is an art as well as a craft and good writing is a subject that has been addressed thoroughly in many well-loved books. So here I'm just touching on a few of the finer points which I've found very useful in marketing writing.

- **Avoid clichés, jargon, slang expressions, and colloquialisms**: Especially if you're writing for an international audience, readers who speak other languages and come from other cultures may be very confused by non-standard expressions. Opt for straightforward language that communicates with precision. An exception is if you're writing for a narrower audience (like urban teenagers in the U.S.) and want to speak their language.

- **Rely on the rule of three**: We humans respond powerfully to certain words, ideas, and patterns. That last sentence was an example of how the three-part sentence is one of those patterns. We're used to digesting information in three-part bites (e.g., "blood, sweat, and tears," "life, liberty, and the pursuit of happiness"). Why is this? Who knows? But it's powerful. So try to limit your sentences to this three-part structure where possible. It becomes harder for readers to digest information in a sentence that includes more than three elements. If there is a long list to be communicated, consider using bullets.

- **Start strong**: Sometimes the communication you write will be part of a marketing campaign with multiple touchpoints. At other times it will have to stand on its own. In either case, write a headline or title and opening sentences that entice the reader to pay attention and keep on reading. I often leave the headline and opening paragraph to the very end or continually fine-tune them as I'm writing the piece and can see what I have.

- **Use the Oxford comma**: This will be my only note on punctuation in this book. The Oxford comma is the final comma in a sentence with a list of items. For example, the Oxford comma is the second comma in this sentence: *I love cookies, ice cream, and donuts.* Some people drop the Oxford comma, which is okay in this last sentence. But in a sentence like this next one, dropping the Oxford comma is awkward to say the least: *This book is dedicated to my parents, Karl Marx and Jesus.* So err on the safe side and always use the Oxford comma!

- **Don't forget that you're selling**: Whether writing a marketing communication about a product, a service, or an idea, always remember that you're employed as a salesperson. Where possible, be sure to clearly mention the product, service, or idea that is the basis of the communication early on. Beyond listing these in the title or headline, you should clarify what the communication is about in the opening sentences or paragraphs so readers don't feel manipulated into reading through lots of content before they understand what you're trying to sell. Being clear upfront is a courtesy. It builds credibility and trust.

Content Optimization Software

Just as robotic writing software is now auto-generating news stories based on corporate earnings reports for the Associated Press and sports reports and recaps for Fox and Yahoo Web sites, there is software that analyzes your writing for its relative effectiveness. For example, Microsoft includes three readability metrics as built-in features of Word (Click the **File** tab, then **Options**, **Proofing**, then under **When correcting spelling and grammar** make sure the **Check grammar with spelling** check box is selected, and select **Show readability statistics**).

When you enable the readability statistics feature after checking the spelling of your document, three data points are displayed.

Readability Statistics	
Counts	
Words	9477
Characters	50300
Paragraphs	298
Sentences	446
Averages	
Sentences per Paragraph	3.2
Words per Sentence	18.5
Characters per Word	5.1
Readability	
Passive Sentences	14%
Flesch Reading Ease	45.4
Flesch-Kincaid Grade Level	11.3
OK	

The Passive Sentences percentage is the first to be displayed. Microsoft flags this because of the belief that sentences written in the active voice are more readable than the passive voice. The higher the percentage, the more passive sentences in the document.

The Flesch Reading Ease score is displayed next. Microsoft explains that the readability score is based on "the average number of syllables per word and words per sentence... This test rates text on a 100-point scale. The higher the score, the easier it is to understand the document. For most standard files, you want the score to be between 60 and 70."

The Flesch-Kincaid Grade Level metric is last. Microsoft explains that this test "rates text on a U.S. school grade level. For example, a score of 8.0 means that an eighth grader can understand the document. For most documents, aim for a score of approximately 7.0 to 8.0."

There are other companies that offer software that does a similar type of writing analysis. Personally, I take these scores with a grain of salt. Great marketing writing involves an element of creativity that can't be written by robots or evaluated using software algorithms. Still, this type of evaluation tends to help reinforce the need for short, succinct sentences that are written in a compelling style, with words that the majority of people can easily understand.

Client Input

After graduating from university with a journalism degree, I felt great pride in my writing skills. So when I started getting feedback from clients on drafts in my first job as an advertising agency copywriter, my first response was defensiveness. This is pretty typical of a young person entering the workforce. But it's completely inappropriate as a marketing, advertising, or public relations writer.

Some clients will absolutely love what you write a lot of the time. Others will turn on Track Changes and remake it into their own style. Most fall somewhere in between. Marketing writing is for the benefit of the client so subtract your ego from the equation. Then strive to understand each edit, critique, or addition.

I've learned that sometimes writing assignments in marketing can involve an iterative process. That is, clients will figure out or hone what they really want to say in a marketing communication only after they see what you come up with—even if you've worked hard at honing a detailed outline that they have approved. In subsequent drafts or iterations, you can help them get closer and closer to their ideal. This is especially true in messaging such as positioning statements and elevator pitches. But the iterative process is common in longer documents like white papers as well.

So approach client input with patience, open-mindedness and an "I want to make you happy" attitude. Sometimes you won't agree with proposed changes. But more often I find that experienced clients provide very intelligent input that usually improves what I've written. Of course if something is grammatically wrong, makes no sense, clashes with something else, or is otherwise incorrect, you should speak up. But in other cases do your best to incorporate edits and suggestions given by clients, paying close attention to whether those changes require still other elements of the piece to change for the sake of consistency and clarity.

Dealing with Difficult Clients

Some clients are very exacting and demanding. This is completely acceptable. But I've also encountered a subset of people within this category who are openly hostile to writers. One theory I have is that these folks may have it in for writers due to a latent desire to write that they never realized. Whatever the reason, these clients will pick apart your copy, looking for any word, phrase, sentence, headline, subhead, or other facet to question or criticize.

How do you handle them? First, the importance of getting a scope of work and outline agreed to up front, before any writing is done, is vital. This, theoretically, binds the client and the writer to content and an organized structure that should not be a surprise. Second, as mentioned in the previous section on going through client input, calmly address each edit, criticism, and suggested revision. Try not to be defensive. If the client crosses the line and becomes abusive, try to focus on getting the job done and let the client know that's your intent. You don't want to work for someone who does not respect you and treats you in a less than businesslike way. Attempt to finish the assignment to the best of your ability and then avoid further work with the person.

In my own experience, if you stick with it and work through whatever changes or edits they would like to make, in the majority of cases these people will become solid advocates for you and your work. Professionalism wins out over difficult people nearly all the time. I call this "mentoring upward," showing people how a professional handles difficult situations with intelligence, grace, and experience to get the job done.

Measuring Your Effectiveness

How do you measure the effectiveness of marketing communications? There are very well-written, amazingly creative, beautifully produced, innovative communications that are unsuccessful. Assuming that the product or service has real value and an opportunity to be successful in the marketplace and is produced with high quality and written well, an unsuccessful marketing communications effort could be due to a lack of proper positioning, weak messaging, or other factors beyond your control.

After your write something, try to get information on how the campaign or individual marketing communication fared. How many inquiries were generated? How many times was a piece of collateral downloaded? How many responses did an email receive? What was the click-through rate on a Web page call-to-action? How much revenue was generated? Getting and sharing this information—especially as part of successful campaigns—will bolster your credentials as an effective content marketing writer.

Marketing and Selling Your Services

Most people writing marketing communications work full time for companies. If you want to freelance, one of the most important first questions to resolve is: How do you successfully market your services? (Of course there are many other questions that freelancers must address, including writing a business plan, incorporation, and tax implications, but they are not covered in this book.)

Writers typically like small spaces to work in, quiet, and privacy. We're not usually champion schmoozers and networkers. So it's not surprising that the thought of how to promote ourselves can occasion feelings of dread and anxiety.

By far the most effective way to get business is through referrals. So tell everyone you know what you're doing. Let the world know online, on your Web site and on social media like LinkedIn and Facebook. Get business cards printed—no, they are not *passé*—that clearly say CONTENT MARKETING WRITER and find opportunities to hand them out.

I was fortunate enough to have a large technology client that has given me ongoing work for nearly 20 years. But even with this company there have been periods of feast and famine. So don't put all of your eggs in one basket. Make sure to continue networking, letting people know that you're available to do work on a project basis.

About the Author

Gene Knauer is a senior content marketing writer and Silicon Valley veteran. He has written for a broad clientele of world-famous technology product and service companies and emerging startups you've never heard of—yet. Content topics span mobile networks; programmable networks; public, private, and hybrid cloud services; hyperscale data centers; Big Data analytics; system on a chip standards; nanotechnology; consulting services; enterprise applications; personal and team productivity software; and much more. His articles have appeared in *American Laboratory*, *Computerworld*, *The Futurist*, the *Los Angeles Times*, *Mobile World Congress Daily*, *Packet Magazine*, and many other trade and corporate publications and newsletters. His clientele has included Autodesk, BEA Systems, Brocade, Cisco Systems, Ericsson, Fujitsu, Microsoft, NTT, Oracle, Sun Microsystems, and VCE.

A graduate of Boston University's Communications School with a degree in journalism, Gene is available as a content marketing writer on a project or retainer basis and as a guest speaker for marketing events http://www.knauer-inc.com.

Check out Gene's blog for content marketing writers https://geneknauer.wordpress.com/.

Acknowledgements

A special thank you to the terrific graphic designer Briana Schweizer and my writer colleagues Joanie Wexler and David Barry.

www.ingramcontent.com/pod-product-compliance
Lightning Source LLC
Chambersburg PA
CBHW071825200526
45169CB00018B/1025